RED DRESS ENERGY

A WOMAN'S GUIDE to EMBRACING HER 7 MAGICAL SUPER-POWERS

BECOME UN-STOPPABLE, UN-BREAKABLE & UN-FORGETTABLE

MICHELLE KULP

Copyright © 2020 Michelle Kulp

Monarch Crown Publishing

All Rights Reserved. No part of this book may be reproduced in any form without permission in writing from the author. Reviewers may quote brief passages in reviews.

ISBN: 978-1-7354188-3-4

Table of Contents

RED DRESS ENERGY i

INTRODUCTION 1

SUPERPOWER #1: THE POWER OF KNOW 21

SUPERPOWER #2 – THE OBSTACLE IS THE HIGHWAY 31

SUPERPOWER #3 – EMBRACE THE MOLT 41

SUPERPOWER #4 – THE POWER OF SIMMERING 49

SUPERPOWER #5 – THE LOST ART OF WANTING 57

SUPERPOWER #6 – DREAM BIG, START SMALL 67

SUPERPOWER #7 – DOUBLE-JUMPING 83

CLOSING THOUGHTS 91

RED DRESS ENERGY

After she established a loving, trusting, and supportive connection with this young part of herself, amazing things began to happen in Linda's life. She reclaimed the playfulness, vitality, and joy that her five-year-old-self had naturally embodied, but that had been locked away by trauma for so long – it hadn't felt safe to go there.

The little Linda had loved to dress up in fancy dresses and a variety of colors. The adult Linda reclaimed this playfulness. One day, she walked into my office, regally as she did now, slid all the way into the depth of the chair, leaned back comfortably, and gave me her signature mischievous smile. She shared, sparkly and giddy with excitement, that she had worn a **Red** sleeveless dress to a party.

She felt like a queen.

She received endless compliments and felt beautiful, joyful, and vibrant. She reflected to me afterward that before this healing, she would never have considered wearing a sleeveless dress, ever. She had been so ashamed of her arms and her body, and she had felt a need to hide it, to shrink from attention. She had felt unsafe.

To wear a **Red Dress** that drew the attention of the entire room had been unthinkable.

And yet, there she was.

She took this **Red Dress Energy** into her board meetings and into her leadership at work. She began to get visible and speak up. She took up space in the room, with her body and with her voice. She was no longer afraid to command attention. She felt her input mattered and it was now finally being received. She was able to be kind and compassionate toward herself, and this translated into other people being kinder and more compassionate with her. The "difficult" people on her team became less difficult. She was more effective as a leader, and she certainly enjoyed herself much more. The dread she used to feel about going to work was replaced with excitement...

Gone was the slumping, shrinking energy that expressed, Don't look at me, don't listen to a single thing I say. I don't belong here. I don't deserve to take up space. I'm ashamed of my being and the way it inconveniences everybody. There is no room for me in this world. Her new royal, queenly energy expressed, I am a gift. My contributions are valuable. I belong here. I'm safe. I'm welcomed I'm loved.

— Excerpt from the book: *Patriarchy Stress Disorder: The Invisible Barrier to Women's Happiness and Fulfillment* by Dr. Valerie Rein

INTRODUCTION

When I was a little girl, I loved to play dress up. I wore princess gowns, carried around magic wands, sprinkled glitter on everything, and embraced my magical powers that transported me to imaginary places where I was the Queen of my very own Queendom.

I used these creative energies to write stories, poetry, and draw pictures of made-up places where everything was vibrant, alive, and enchanted.

As I got older, I traded in my *magical mojo* and began to conform to who I *thought* I should be instead of who I *actually* was. My authentic self remained locked away for many years. Over time, my real self became a distant memory.

The Secondary Dream

At 17 years old, I was sitting in a Business Law class and declared my forever career path – I would become an attorney. I loved the idea of being a part of the justice system and having the power and privilege to help others who had been unfairly victimized; I wanted to wave my magic wand and transform wrongs into rights.

I never did achieve that dream of becoming an attorney. Instead, I went down an alternate path of getting married, raising three children and becoming a paralegal. I remained in that career for 17 years… until I couldn't breathe any longer.

In the beginning, I was passionately in love with my legal career, but over time, it drained me mentally, spiritually, emotionally, and physically.

I started feeling extraordinary amounts of stress, anxiety, and unfulfillment at my job. I felt like I was in Job Prison because the environment was stifling, suffocating, oppressive, and at times, unjust.

How Long Can You Fake It?

Even though I loved playing make believe as a young girl, doing it as an adult was a completely different story. One day I decided that I could no longer "fake" being happy in a career for which I had long ago lost my passion.

After 17 years in the legal field, I had a sickening realization that it wasn't about "justice" or "fairness," but about who had deeper pockets to win these long, drawn out, and draining legal battles.

It was a game with many unwritten rules that took advantage of naïve, inexperienced, and unknowing people.

I played the game because it was a matter of survival but began to fantasize and plan my escape from JOB prison.

I desperately wanted out.

At the darkest time in my life, I had a serendipitous meeting with country music singer and actor Billy Ray Cyrus that CHANGED. EVERY. THING.

The **Red Dress** That Changed My Life

Yes, that's me with Billy Ray Cyrus after a concert in 1992. I was 29 years old. This meeting was a pivotal moment in my life, so I want to share this transformational story with you...

My Pivotal Moment

On October 23, 1992, I met a man named Billy Ray Cyrus (Country Music Singer and Actor), who changed the entire trajectory of my life. Some might say it was merely a coincidence, but I strongly believe it was my spiritual destiny.

In 1992, I was in a very dark and desperate place in my life. My marriage had recently ended; I was raising three children (then ages 1, 3, and 5) on my own with no financial or emotional support from my ex-husband. I was let go at the law firm where I had worked for several years and was living cut-off notice to cut-off notice. My older brother and best friend, Michael, had been diagnosed with AIDS and was dying. I started having chest pains that brought me to the emergency room, where I was hooked up to an EKG machine to see what was going on. The doctors discovered it wasn't my heart, but rather "panic attacks" brought on by "chronic stress."

Music That Spoke to My Soul

After I left my highly toxic, abusive, and dysfunctional marriage, I rented a small townhouse. One evening, my neighbor stopped by and asked me if I had ever heard of Billy Ray Cyrus. Until that point in my life, I had only listened to rock-n-roll music, having grown up on 80's rock music and marrying a drummer in a rock band; I was not interested or familiar with country music. My neighbor gave me a tape of Billy Ray's music and weirdly encouraged me to listen to it, especially the song "Achy Breaky Heart." I quickly got hooked on this very addictive tune. Many nights, I blasted that song and danced around my townhouse with my three young children, who also loved the song. It was a wonderful escape from my very stressed out life!

A couple of weeks later, my neighbor reappeared to tell me that Billy Ray Cyrus was playing at a concert on October 23, 1992 at the Patriot Center in Fairfax, Virginia, and she encouraged me to attend. If it had been October 22nd or October 24th, I wouldn't have thought twice about it, but because it was October 23rd — my birthday — I felt it had a special meaning. In fact, the thought instantly popped into my head, "Billy Ray is playing on my birthday because he has something very important to tell me that is going to change my life." Perhaps due to all the stress I was under, I had become delusional, but I honestly believed with every fiber of my being that I was going to meet Billy Ray Cyrus and he had something important to tell me.

No Doubts, But Lots of Obstacles

Because I was 100% certain that I would meet Billy Ray, I purchased two tickets to his concert and recruited one of my adventurous friends to attend. The plan was simple: I would wear a **RED DRESS** to stand out from the crowd and then try to get backstage after the concert. I had done this in my teenage years and met famous musicians like David Lee Roth and Eddie Van Halen (RIP Eddie). So, I figured my musician-meeting plan would work again.

After four failed attempts to get backstage, my friend and I were kicked out of the Patriot Center and told we would be arrested if we returned. We immediately went to Plan B, which was to wait for Billy Ray to come out and follow his limo to the hotel where he was staying.

An hour or so later, Billy Ray finally appeared from a tunnel underneath the Patriot Center; he was signing autographs and videotaping his fans...he adored his fans! We stayed in our car, ready to follow the limo. We weren't the only ones who had this bright idea. Hundreds of women were prepared to follow the limo for a tiny chance to meet the very handsome and talented Billy Ray Cyrus. This did not discourage me in the least. I drove like a maniac so I wouldn't lose sight of the limo, cutting off other drivers and running red lights, blindly following Billy Ray's limo as well as my dreams!

I Would NOT Give Up

We followed the limo to the Hilton Hotel, where Billy Ray's bodyguard, Steve, was directing Billy Ray to his hotel room through a side door. Luckily for me, all the other women who were following the limo jumped out of their cars and ran towards the hotel's side door. My friend jumped out of our moving car and went inside to tell Billy Ray to wait for me because it was my birthday. I illegally parked the car in a handicapped space and ran to the elevator where Billy Ray was standing inside, surrounded by a sea of women. Billy Ray locked eyes on me (the **Red Dress** stood out!) as he took my hand and pulled me inside the elevator, I told Billy Ray it was my birthday! Just then, the bodyguard snapped a picture of us, Billy Ray autographed a tee-shirt and a book I was carrying (*Creative Visualization* by Shakti Gawain), then handed me a red rose for my birthday. Maybe all the adrenaline caused me to have crazy thoughts, but I felt a special chemistry with Billy Ray. Unfortunately, before I could do or say anything, bodyguard Steve pushed me out of the elevator and told everyone, "Billy Ray is going upstairs now. Good night!"

At that moment, the elevator doors closed not only on me but on my dreams! I knew that whatever my friend and I did, the other women would do as well, so we had to get rid of our competition. We *faked* leaving the hotel and drove around the parking lot. Within 10 minutes, all the other women had cleared out, so we went back into the hotel. I wasn't about to give up on my dream of meeting Billy Ray Cyrus; after all, he had something important to tell me that would change my life. So, we got back into the elevator and pushed the buttons for every floor. I thought maybe the hotel would have blocked the floor that Billy Ray was staying on, but they didn't – all the lights lit up!

The Search

Starting on the top floor, we got off the elevator and looked down the hall for clues of Billy Ray. It didn't take us long to find the floor he was staying on. I looked down the hall and saw the bodyguard, Steve, go into the last room. I was so excited! Finally, my dream was coming true! As I approached the hotel room, bodyguard Steve heard me and came out to inform me that if I didn't leave, he was going to call hotel security and have me removed. I thought I could sweet-talk him into letting me see Billy Ray, but the more I talked, the more irritated and annoyed he became with me. I made up stories, then argued with him for a while until my friend told me she didn't want to get arrested and thought we better listen to Steve and leave. I hesitantly headed back towards the elevator.

Obstacles Will Not Stop Me

I was so close to having my dreams come true. I could feel it in my bones. The only thing standing between Billy Ray and me was the hallway, and I was not going to let a *hallway* come between me and my dreams.

I decided, come hell or high water, I would figure out a way to meet Billy Ray Cyrus even if I had to camp out and sleep on the floor by the elevator and wait for him to come out of his hotel room in the morning. As we stood there, I searched my mind for anything that would get me closer to Billy Ray. I looked up and noticed a small sign that had the room numbers printed on it, which read something like "Rooms 1200-1223" with an arrow pointing towards the direction I saw the bodyguard go in. I looked across the hall and noticed a house phone on a table. I picked up the phone and dialed the last number on the sign and Voila! Billy Ray answered the phone (apparently, the bodyguard was staying in a separate room across the hall).

When Billy Ray answered the phone and asked who was calling, I told him it was the "Birthday Girl," to which he replied, "You mean the girl in the **Red Dress**?" Wow! I couldn't believe it! Billy Ray remembered me because of my **Red Dress**! He told me he had something to say to me that I wasn't going to believe." Curiously, I waited for his explanation. He said that if there hadn't been all those women in the elevator, he would have invited me to his hotel room for some Chinese food. I told him, "I'm here now!"

Better Late Than Never

Billy Ray explained that he hurt his back onstage, and a masseuse was coming to his room shortly, but I could come to see him afterward. My girlfriend did not want to wait, so I gave Billy Ray my phone number (this was before cell phones) to our hotel and told him to call me when he was done.

A couple of hours went by with no call from Billy Ray.

It was getting late, so I finally changed out of my **Red Dress** and into my pajamas, but I left my hair and make-up intact just in case Billy Ray called. About 2:00 am, I was listening to Billy Ray's music, still on an adrenaline high, when the phone in my hotel room finally rang and it was Billy Ray! He asked me what my birthday wish was. I quickly told him, "To meet and talk to you in person." He said if it wasn't too late, he would love it if I would come over to his hotel for a visit. I hung up the phone, put on my **Red Dress** and was speeding down the highway towards his hotel within minutes.

Dreams Do Come True

I arrived back at the Hilton Hotel and was walking down the hallway toward Billy Ray's room when bodyguard Steve heard me and came out to investigate. He told me to leave the hotel immediately before he called hotel security and the police. I swore to him that Billy Ray had called me and invited me to his room. I'm sure he heard that line all the time from Billy Ray's female fans. Luckily, Billy Ray's room door was slightly ajar, and the bodyguard stepped into his room and asked him if what I said was true. Billy Ray confirmed what I told him, so Steve had no choice but to let me in.

I spent the next few hours talking to Billy Ray (he was a complete gentleman). We spoke about our lives, our families, relationships, etc. He had a very spiritually enlightened side to him, a stark contrast from his "stage" persona. He shared that some people called him an "overnight success" despite the fact that he spent more than ten years playing in bars to become this so-called "overnight success." I told Billy Ray my rather desperate life story, and he looked deeply into my eyes and said something that changed my entire life…

The Life-Changing Question

Billy Ray asked me, *"What are your dreams?"* I replied, *"I don't have any dreams. My life's about survival."* Billy Ray assured me I had a dream and that I should discover what that dream was and never, ever give up on it. In fact, he made me promise I would never give up on my dream once I found it.

One Year, One Small Book, and One BIG Dream!

I took Billy Ray's advice and spent the next year searching for this elusive dream. It wasn't so easy to find. I read books and talked to people, but I could not figure out what it was. I started feeling sorry for myself thinking, *"Everyone has a dream except me. What's wrong with me?"*

Then, one day I was at Borders Bookstore (sadly, they went out of business) when a tiny book, *How to Find Your Mission in Life* by Richard Bolles, fell into my hands and gave me the answer I was searching for. The author also wrote another popular book you may know titled *What Color is Your Parachute?* The one question that helped me discover my dream was:

"What do you love to do where you lose all sense of time?"

Finally! I knew the answer – I loved to write! When I was young, I would write for hours and hours, and time would fly by. When I was writing, five hours seemed like five minutes to me. I knew writing was my dream because I had absolutely no concept of time when I was lost in my writing.

One Road Leads to Many Others

In 1993, I headed down that road toward my dream – to become a writer. I joined writers' groups, attended writers' conferences, and read every book about writing I could get my hands on. Then, I wrote a manuscript titled *"Woman, Take Hold of Your Power: 50 Unconscious Ways Women Give Away Their Power"* and tried for over a year to get a publishing deal. I received rejection letter after rejection letter and was becoming quite discouraged.

Finally, one day a prominent New York publishing house called and said they wanted to ask me some questions about my manuscript. I was so excited! I thought to myself, "Thank you, God, my dreams are finally coming true!"

Since the manuscript I submitted was for a self-help book for women, the editor wanted to know my "credentials."

Credentials? Huh?

He went on to ask me if I had a Ph.D. "No, I have something better than a Ph.D." I told him.

He curiously asked, "What could be better than a Ph.D.?"

"Life experience."

I didn't write that book from theory, but from my own real-life stories and personal experiences, and those of my friends."

The big publishing house editor didn't quite agree with me and informed me that *life experience* wasn't going to cut it. He said, "Unfortunately, the publishing business is very competitive, and unless you have a Ph.D., we cannot take a chance on an unknown author. It's just business. I hope you understand."

I hung up the phone feeling disappointed and excited at the same time. Disappointed that they weren't going to publish my book but excited that I finally had confirmation from a highly credible source that my writing was *good enough* to *almost* get published.

I never did get that manuscript published by a traditional publisher, but several years later I fulfilled my dream when I self-published my book on Amazon.

How I Reverse-Engineered Getting Writing Credentials

After discovering that writing was my dream (thank you, Billy Ray and Richard Bolles), I believed I needed these "writing credentials" the editor spoke of during that phone call.

I decided I would become a newspaper reporter to get these *credentials*. Since I didn't have a degree in journalism, I had to get creative to get a job as a newspaper reporter.

My plan was hatched...

I would become a "FAKE" reporter, and my writing would be so amazing that the newspaper would have to hire me.

So, with my "FAKE" credentials, I attended local events where I interviewed people, took pictures, and wrote stories. It was a lot of fun! I felt like an actress starring in a movie; I was convincing myself that I was a real reporter.

Once I finished writing my first article, I asked my father (who told me the editor of the newspaper walked to work every morning on the same path) to give my story and pictures to the editor.

Being my biggest fan and supporter, my father agreed to approach the editor on his way to work. The next day, he handed him a yellow envelope, which included my typewritten story and pictures. He told the editor, "My daughter asked me to give this to you."

That was it.

About a week later, my very first story was published on the front page of the local newspaper and I was ecstatic! At this point, I had not spoken with the editor. I was basking in the feeling of seeing my "byline" in this newspaper article and felt like I was now a *real writer*. After all I had *credentials*!

I repeated this process for four weeks, and every week, my articles were prominently published in the newspaper. Finally, the editor called me, and in a slightly irritated voice, he asked me, "What do you want? A job or something?"

John, the editor, was a large, tall, intimidating, and controversial man from Scotland that people seemed to either love or hate. I found out later that he liked it that way.

I told him that I *might* want a job, so he invited me into the office to speak to him.

When I arrived at the newspaper headquarters, he asked me to shut the office door so no one could hear our conversation. He annoyingly stated, "You see all those reporters out there? Well, I have to do a lot of editing when they turn in their stories!"

I timidly replied, "Isn't' that what editors do?"

"Yes, but my point is your writing is good, and I didn't have to edit much of it."

Wow! What a compliment! I was floored, to say the least. Not long after that, he offered me a full-time position as a reporter.

Unfortunately, when I learned that the salary was half of what I was making as a paralegal, I had to decline his gracious offer. Thankfully, we made a deal that I would work as a freelance reporter for the newspaper instead, and he would pay me per article and per picture. It was perfect because as a freelancer, I could now get all the "writing credentials" I needed while creating a new income stream to support myself and my three children. I remained a freelance reporter for almost three years.

My dream of becoming a writer led to many other roads I would have never imagined myself on – I became a motivational speaker, a workshop leader, an online entrepreneur, a book launch expert, and of course, a published author.

It's hard to believe I am a speaker since I spent seven long years overcoming an intense fear of public speaking (that's a whole other book). Thank you, Toastmasters and Speaking Circles®.

Deep down, however, I knew that if I was ever going to become a successful writer, I had to get over my fear of public speaking. I mistakenly believed I was being judged harshly by others and didn't feel worthy enough to share my voice with the world. I finally overcame that fear and now happily share my story on stage in front of hundreds and sometimes thousands of people.

Listening to My Inner Voice Helped Me Not Only Survive, But Thrive

Instead of listening to my fears that were keeping me safe and small, I began listening to my SOUL. I started to appreciate my resourcefulness, creativity, determination, ability to think outside the box, and my risk-taking skills, which some people referred to as "insanity."

Living My Dream

I am living the life I dreamed of many years ago. I have a fulfilling online business that I love. I work 20-25 hours a week, I have freedom and flexibility, and a multiple 6-figure income. I have been publishing a book a month since January 2020 and am now close to making a full-time income solely from my writing.

My life drastically changed when I decided to wear the Red Dress to the concert so I could meet Billy Ray Cyrus.

Deciding to wear a **Red Dress** so I could stand out took a lot of courage that I didn't possess at the time, considering I was self-conscious, introverted, shy, insecure, and didn't like attention. Luckily, my desperate plot in life, along with my obsession about meeting Billy Ray won out and I didn't give in to all those fears. After all, I was sinking, and I needed a life raft to save me.

If you've ever worn a **Red Dress**, you know the powerful energy that goes along with it. This energy is bold, audacious, confident, fearless, and daring.

Red Dress Energy vs. Big DOG Energy

When I told my 30-year-old daughter the title of this book, before I even started writing it, she asked, "Is RDE the same as BDE?"

I had forgotten about that term until she reminded me. In case you haven't heard that term before, I'll share one of the milder definitions of BDE which is *"Big Dog Energy"*; if you Google the term, you will see other unrefined definitions.

Below are the five characteristics of *Big Dog Energy (BDE):*

1. You don't need to explain yourself. Your greatness speaks volumes on its own.

2. You influence people without even trying.

3. You show, rather than tell.

4. Your confidence is unparalleled, yet calm.

5. You're not easily rattled by the opinions of others.

Here are the five characteristics I created for **Red Dress Energy:**

1. You use your intuitive, flawless, embodied GPS that knows the right direction for you. You own and trust your next step(s), and you say YES to yourself!

2. You honor your MOJO that transforms darkness into light. MOJO is that fire in your belly, light in your eyes, and wildly beating heart. It's STAR Power.

3. You embrace your Inner Rebel and Warrior, which rejects the status quo; you embrace living life on your terms. You follow the path of an independent thinker.

4. You honor your JOY, intentions, visions, and dreams. You don't conform or fall for tempting traps.

5. You fall down seven times and get up eight. Obstacles are expected, and you are okay with that.

Having **RDE** is not about boasting about how great, brilliant, smart, funny, or successful you are; your actions speak louder than words. It's about tapping into that inner MOJO we all have, that Queenly Energy every girl is born with; it's about being your natural, authentic, and unapologetic self.

RDE is having laser focus to birth your dreams and not allowing anyone or anything to get in your way, not even the saboteur that lives within you.

You don't settle for crumbs or half dreams, you want. It. All. On. Your. Terms.

I'm writing this book to remind myself and YOU, my reader, that we all have this *Hidden Power* that lives inside us because we are ALL born with it. It fades away over time as we conform to society, culture, our families, and the expectations of others.

It's time to start tapping into your own **Red Dress Energy** and breathe new life into it. Let the fun begin!

I've come up with Seven Superpowers that will help you tap into your own **RDE**…

SUPERPOWER #1
THE POWER OF KNOW

*You can't be what you can't see,
and you can't have what you can't see.*

In 2000, I had been renting a house for myself and my three children for about five years when the landlord suddenly told me that, due to health issues, he had to sell the house and asked me if I was interested in purchasing it.

I was broke, living paycheck-to-paycheck, and getting help from my parents and the church to pay my bills. "No, I'm not interested in purchasing your house. I have no money."

It wasn't my dream house anyway, so I had no burning desire to buy that house, but I needed to quickly figure out where my children and I would live.

One day, as I was driving to Walmart, I saw a new development being built with enormous, beautiful homes and perfectly manicured lawns. I also saw a massive price tag on the sign in front of the model home, but I still wanted to see what this *unattainable* house looked like inside.

Love at First Sight

I fell madly in love the minute I walked through the front door; like I was under a magic spell. At that moment, I knew I had to have this house.

Now remember, I was flat broke, could barely pay my bills, and there was no possible way I could get a loan for this house.

Even though my mind couldn't come up with a logical, step-by-step plan to attain my dream house, I also believed in the power of faith and miracles. I've kept a miracle jar for years to remind me that miracles happen all the time. So, I chose to focus on miracles happening.

I had a deep, unwavering faith that "this or something better" would come to fruition.

For the next several weeks, I visited the model home and imagined myself and my children living there. I would spend hours at the model home, in different rooms, seeing and feeling myself living there. I knew the salespeople on a first name basis, and I think they liked my company, so they let me hang out in my fantasy home.

I was convinced without a doubt that this was my dream home, and so I wouldn't accept anything less.

I told my younger brother about my housing dilemma, and he said he wanted to help me. He generously offered to put a down payment on a home for the kids and me, but not that one since it was way beyond what I could afford.

So, we began looking at other homes. Nothing measured up to this model home, though. I drove my real estate agent crazy as she showed me house after house to no avail.

Time was running out. I was going to be homeless in less than a month if I didn't find a house to buy.

Something in my gut told me not to settle. There were a lot of houses I could *afford*, but they didn't excite me.

At the last minute, a new house came on the market. I went to see it, and it was the exact layout of the model home, just a bit smaller. It wasn't brand new, but it looked brand new with all the updates. Most importantly, it had a price tag I could afford. My brother put down $60,000 so I could get this house, and within a short time, I moved into my new dream home.

I raised my kids in this beautiful home, and looking back, I realize that would never have happened if I had not become completely obsessed with that model home.

I showed up at that model home several times a week and "acted" like I owned the place. It felt real to me, just like when I was a young girl pretending to be Dorothy from *The Wizard of Oz*.

When We KNOW, We KNOW

It wasn't until I was desperate and in enough pain that I learned to trust my inner knowing, even when what I saw with my physical eyes looked completely different.

In the book, *Women Who Run with the Wolves*, author Clarissa Pinkola Estes, Ph.D., says:

> *From the time we are born, there is a wildish urge within us that desires our souls lead our lives, for the ego can only understand so much. Imagine the ego on a permanent and relatively short leash; it can only go so far into the mysteries of life and spirit.*

Our souls have a homing device, and when we allow ourselves to tap into it, we will find our way home to our true selves, our true desires, and our inner knowing.

A Sign That Your Ego Is Leading Your Life Is That It Demands Facts and Strict Proof

When it came to the facts about getting that dream home, my ego-mind was saying, "Michelle, you can't afford that house; you should be practical and appreciative that your brother is helping you. Pick a *good enough house* (code for *Settle for less than what you want* and *Don't rock the boat*.) However, my soul was screaming, "Michelle, you can have your dream house. You can have whatever you set your heart, mind, and soul on. Miracles happen. Don't give up on your dreams."

Wayne Dyer once said:

When you are in spirit, you are inspired.

I was inspired by the model home. I was *not* inspired by the house I was living in or any of the houses my agent was showing me.

This is when I started practicing the art of allowing. I allowed mystery and synchronicity into my life and believed that everything I needed would come to me at precisely the right time.

When I'm operating from my soul, wild synchronicities begin to show up; like the house I ended up buying having the exact layout of the model home! Like my brother loaning me $60,000 to buy a house at the exact moment I needed. Like my dream house going on the market at the last minute.

How Do You Trust Your Knowing When Everything Else Is Saying the Opposite?

Go back to your childhood and get in touch with that level of belief you had when you played imaginary games.

When I lived in Milford, Connecticut, my best friend, Karen, lived next door, and we were inseparable. We played Barbies for hours underneath the apple tree in her front yard, and we loved to pretend we were characters from our favorite movie, *The Wizard of Oz*.

I grew up with three brothers, so I loved having my best friend, Karen, next door; she was like a sister, and we loved spending the night at each other's houses.

I had a small, carved wooden box my parents bought me that Karen and I called our "wish box." Whatever we wrote down on a piece of paper and put in our "wish box," we believed 100% it would come true.

Our belief level was maxed out! Whenever we wanted our parents to say *yes* to things like spending the night, we would write it down on a piece of paper and put it in our wish box. We would send good energy all day long that our parents would let us spend the night, and most of the time, our wishes came true!

If You Had a Wish Box That Could Grant Your Biggest Wish, What Would That Be?

Go back to your younger self and forget about other people's expectations, obligations, bills, demands, and allow yourself to dream big for a moment. Go into that childlike fantasy thinking where there are no limits.

When I decided I was going to meet Billy Ray Cyrus, my friends thought I was batsh*t crazy and some suggested I might need to go to a mental health facility and get help. Granted, it was a desperate and dark time in my life, but my soul was speaking so loudly to me, I had to ignore my ego and everyone else who told me I was nuts!

I had the most profound knowing I've ever had that I would meet Billy Ray Cyrus and he would change my life. Forever.

Without that meeting, I believe I would still be stuck working at the law firm in a job I hated, which was sucking the life out of me. I'd be part of the "walking dead"; a lifeless zombie.

Don't Listen to the Dark Gods

In her book, *Inspired and Unstoppable*, author Tama Kieves tells a story about how she was attending a writer's conference when she met Mr. Big Publishing, who said to her, *"If a book doesn't do well in the first six months, we just punt."*

She goes on to explain:

Later I realized it wasn't just his choice of words that bothered me. It was his tone. That know-it-all, this-is-reality, this-is-the-only reality tone. It was a dominance that made belief seem like a lapse in sound judgment and faith seem impotent and desperate, like some yellow butterfly in a machine shop. In a matter-of-fact way, he said something that was not a matter of fact: that if something didn't succeed in the first six months, it wouldn't ever be a media darling or turn heads.

Mr. Big Publishing is what I have come to call a Dark God. They are people who speak with false certainty and represent, "the world." They stand square with their hands on their hips, claim authority, and suck up all the oxygen around them… These Dark Gods can dismiss your world with a single comment, and feel justified, accurate, and even philanthropic in their presumptions.

Don Miguel Ruiz, bestselling author of *The Four Agreements*, calls these types of people something similar – **Black Magicians**. He says, "One word is like a spell, and humans use the words like **Black Magicians**, thoughtlessly putting spells on each other."

Everyone has **Dark Gods** preventing them from living their dreams and claiming their desires.

Name three *Dark Gods* in your life right now:

1. _____

2. _____

3. _____

We are all suckers for authority. We were raised to respect authority and to put other people's thoughts, opinions, and judgments ahead of our own.

When that big NY publishing house rejected my manuscript many years ago, I could have let that be the end of my dreams, except I didn't.

When bodyguard Steve told me, "Billy Ray is going upstairs for the night…" I could have let that be the end of my dreams, except I didn't.

As I look back, the bodyguard spoke with complete authority because his job was to prevent fans like me from getting too close to Billy Ray. Also, he probably just wanted to get some sleep. I ignored this **Dark God** and turned my obstacles into a new path that ultimately got me what I wanted – a meeting with Billy Ray!

Please don't let **Dark Gods** block you from your dreams. When you are committed to realizing your dream, you will achieve it no matter what.

I'm not saying there won't be obstacles; there absolutely will. As soon as you commit to your dreams, the obstacles will show up.

This leads us to the next chapter... why *Obstacles* are the HIGHWAY to your DREAMS.

SUPERPOWER #2
THE OBSTACLE IS THE HIGHWAY

In his bestselling book, *The Obstacle is the Way*, Ryan Holiday, says:

> This thing in front of you. This issue. This obstacle – this frustrating, unfortunate, problematic, unexpected problem preventing you from doing what you want to do. That thing you dread or secretly hope will never happen. What if it wasn't so bad.
>
> What if embedded inside it or inherent in it were certain benefits – benefits only for you? What would you do? What do you think most people would do?
>
> Probably what they've always done, and what you are doing right now: NOTHING.
>
> Let's be honest. Whatever our individual goals, most of us sit frozen before the many obstacles that lie ahead of us.

Obstacles Are Launching Pads to New and Improved Plans

You can view an obstacle as either a stop sign that will end your dreams OR a slight detour. It's you who decides.

Every obstacle we encounter in life is an opportunity to improve our condition if we allow it to.

What Is Holding You Back from Your Dreams Right Now?

- You're too old?
- You're too young?
- You're too inexperienced?
- You're too broke?
- You lack support?
- You're feeling uncertain?
- You're afraid?
- You lack the resources?
- Self-doubt?
- You don't like confrontation?
- You're shy?
- You don't like going outside of your comfort zones?

Obstacles are Teachers

Obstacles show up to teach you how to get where you want to go by carving a new path and developing the exact characteristics and traits you need to achieve those things.

It's easy to think the "enemy" is outside of us, trying to block our dreams and goals. But the truth is **WE ARE THE ENEMY** – our learned helplessness, our fears, frustrations, our not wanting to rock the boat. Where one person sees a crisis or obstacle, another sees an opportunity.

Ryan Holiday Says There Are Three Disciplines to Overcoming Obstacles:

1. Perception

2. Action

3. Will

I think back to my Billy Ray Cyrus adventure and know it would have been easy for me to give up.

Instead, I took ACTION in the face of the challenges and the intensity of my WILL helped me overcome:

1. Being kicked out of the Patriot Center four times.

2. Driving in the dark, late at night (before cell phones and before GPS), blindly following a limousine.

3. Competing with other female fans vying for his attention.

4. Being kicked out of the elevator.

5. The bodyguard threatening to call hotel security and the police.

6. My friend asking me not to argue with the bodyguard.

7. Leaving the situation and not knowing what to do next.

8. Being asked to wait until Billy Ray addressed his back issues.

9. Not knowing the way back to his hotel once Billy Ray called.

10. Another confrontation with the bodyguard when I did get back to the hotel at 2:30 a.m.

I could have allowed any of these obstacles to stop me.

What if I had given up when the bodyguard threatened to call hotel security even though Billy Ray had invited me to his room?

My **COMPLETE OBSESSION** allowed me to ignore all the obstacles and keep moving forward to achieve my goal. Billy Ray even acknowledged my determination and strength when I was in his hotel room, saying, "You're a very strong and determined lady. You overcame a lot to get here."

Outward Appearances Can Be Deceptive

We need to remember that our brains are hardwired to detect threats and dangers, and my brain was no different that night. All those events were a threat to my safety and could have been perceived as dangerous.

But I didn't give in to those fears and threats; I just kept focusing on what I believed wholeheartedly – that meeting Billy Ray Cyrus would change my life forever and for the better.

We Aren't Powerless

We get to decide what we will make of every situation we encounter in our lives. Will we give up after one obstacle? How about three obstacles? 10 obstacles? 100 obstacles?

What's your IQ? Your I.Quit. moment?

I didn't have one I.Quit moment that night. If the bodyguard had not let me in Billy Ray's room, I probably would have hatched another plan, or I would have camped out at the elevator because I knew Billy Ray would eventually have to come out of his hotel room.

Our mind is a trickster, and it wants to keep us safe and locked up in a prison instead of out in the world fighting for what we want.

Now you might be wondering… "Michelle, why do I have to fight for what I want? Shouldn't it come naturally and easily?"

I don't know of any great goals and dreams I have achieved in my life that came without a lot of obstacles.

It's as If the Obstacles Are Built Into the Goals

It knows who we have to *become* to reach the goal. And perhaps we're being tested by the Universe to see how badly we want what we say we want.

If we give up after a few obstacles, we weren't very serious about it, were we?

Think about a time when you felt powerless and paralyzed and gave up on your goal. How many obstacles did you encounter before you quit?

I want you to pick a goal that you gave up on and write down the obstacles you faced and identify the one that made you quit?

My Boss Wouldn't Allow Me to Quit

After I left the legal field, I took a job in outside sales because it offered me the possibility to work half the hours and make twice the income (six figures).

At the beginning of my sales career, I wasn't making much money in this 100% commission job, so I tried to quit several times.

My manager, Bob, would listen to my complaints and assure me that there was a one-year learning curve, and once the learning period was over, he said I was going to be a "sales superstar."

The fact was, he believed in me more than I believed in myself at the time.

It's naïve to think there won't be obstacles when we have any type of worthy goal. Obstacles always show up to teach us the lessons we need to learn.

And guess what? After my first year in outside sales, I made what the average salesperson made – $60,000 – working 20-25 hours per week. Then, in my second year, I hit six figures! Bob was right. I just had to give it time and trust that it would all work out.

- What if I had quit in that first year?
- What if I didn't have a manager that believed in me and kept encouraging me to move forward?
- What if my insecurities and fears took over and I went back to the false security of a miserable job in the legal field working 40+ hours making $50k per year?

I wouldn't be here making multiple six figures doing what I love right now.

REPETITION IS THE KEY

Think about something you are really good at, that you have mastered. Did you master that skill the first time you tried it? I doubt it. It takes repetition to get to mastery.

A woodpecker can tap on a thousand trees a dozen times and get nowhere. Or, he can tap ten thousand times on one tree and get dinner!

To achieve our dreams and goals, we must be willing to keep tapping until we get what we want.

That can be very uncomfortable, but the life we want lives just beyond our comfort zones.

In his book, *Think Like a Monk*, Jay Shetty says:

> *A few decades ago, scientists conducted an experiment in the Arizona desert where they built "Biosphere 2 – a huge steel-and-glass enclosure with air that had been purified, clean water, nutrient-rich soil and lots of natural light. It was meant to provide ideal living conditions for the flora and fauna within. And while successful in some ways, it was an absolute failure. Over and over, when trees inside the Biosphere grew to a certain height, they would simply fall over. At first, the phenomenon confused scientists. Finally, they realized that the Biosphere lacked a key element necessary to the trees' health:* **WIND**.
>
> *The* **WIND** *is what causes the trees to respond to that PRESSURE and AGITATION by growing stronger bark and deeper roots that ultimately increases their stability.*
>
> *We humans waste a lot of time trying to stay in our comfort zones and the bubble of our self-made Biospheres. What we don't realize is, it's those obstacles and challenges that make us stronger and more resilient.*

Welcome the obstacles in your life because they are working to make you stronger and more resilient so you can get everything your heart desires.

Obstacles Are the Highway to Your Dream Life

Think of obstacles you've overcome, whether internal or external. One huge benefit of overcoming obstacles is that it boosts your confidence and self-assurance.

I think back to my intense fear of public speaking that took me years to overcome after being in Toastmasters and a facilitator for Speaking Circles®. The confidence I gained from overcoming one of my biggest fears also had an unexpected benefit of spilling over into many areas of my life.

Not only did I gain confidence from being able to speak publicly, but I had more confidence in my relationships, in dealing with confrontations, in business, and so much more!

You don't need to avoid obstacles; just know they are there for many unknown reasons, and you will grow tremendously when you overcome them.

Remember: A worthy goal is full of hidden obstacles; look for the opportunities and stay focused and 100% committed to the goal.

To achieve BIG Dreams and Goals in life, you're going to have to die to your old self so that you can become someone new.

"And no one pours new wine into old wineskins. If he does, the wine will burst the skins, and both the wine and the wineskins will be ruined. Instead, new wine is poured into new wineskins." (Mark 2:22)

When I left my 17-year career as a paralegal, my old identity had to die as I created a new one (a new wineskin).

In the next chapter, we're going to talk about letting go of the old and embracing the new.

SUPERPOWER #3
EMBRACE THE MOLT

Sitting in my therapist's office, bawling and trying to come to terms with the realization that I can't keep doing what I've been doing. *It isn't working anymore, my life is eff'd up, and I'm miserable.*

Dr. Rebecca explained, "Michelle, it's like you've got these old worn-out shoes that you've had for a long time. Your feet have adjusted to them, and they have been comfortable for many years, but now they are worn out, they have holes in the soles, and it's time for a new pair of shoes. Of course, when you get new shoes, it will feel awkward and uncomfortable, but just like your old shoes, eventually, you will adjust to them and you'll love them."

I remember crying even more after she shared this shoe analogy with me because I really wanted to keep my old shoes. It felt like I would be admitting defeat if I agreed to get new shoes, but it wasn't. It was just the cycle of life and time for me to enter a new season in my life.

Lobsters and Many Other Species Molt to Grow

Molting is the shedding of the old to make room for the new.

Lobster shells don't grow. To get bigger, the lobster must ditch its old shell and wait for a new one to harden around its body. A lobster looks like a rubbery toy, and it lives inside the hard shell.

As it molts, it will absorb water and swell to reach its new size. It can grow in weight by 40-50%.

The new shell has everything the old shell had:

- Gills
- Antennae
- Spine
- Mouth parts
- Bristle
- And more

Molting takes place in the safety of a lobster's burrow; when its shell is soft, the lobster is easy prey while waiting for its brand-new shell to strengthen.

After several months, the molting and growing cycle begins again. Lobsters molt quite frequently when they are younger (5-6 times each season) and when they are adults, they molt 1-2 times per year.

Here is a link to an incredible video of a blue crayfish molting: https://youtu.be/WZP1fFKZ2Fs

When crayfish get ready to molt, they find it hard to breathe — probably because their insides are pressed tightly against their exoskeletons.

To molt, they must loosen and eventually extricate their soft insides from their exoskeleton. They literally have to jump or crawl out of their old "skin."

Molting is a regular occurrence for many species, and human beings are no exception. We are not meant to stay the same our entire lives; we're meant to grow and evolve.

Although I fought against *letting go of the old me* (with the old coping mechanisms and beliefs), deep down, I knew it was time.

The good news is no shell is wasted. We can take what we learned in the previous season(s) of our lives and apply it to the new season.

In an article written by Dr. Bryan A. Wilson, he describes four steps of what he calls the **Mental Molt**:

Whether or not experiences we face are positive or negative, we assign mental patterns as leverage when facing new challenges. But what happens when these tools no longer work or serve to elevate you to the next level you're striving for? That's where embracing the molt becomes ever so important. Below I briefly describe a series of steps that detail the mental molt we all must endure to reach higher levels (whatever that means for you).

- *Awareness of Change*
- *Stillness*
- *Vulnerability*
- *Allow Room for Growth*

Awareness of Change

It's important to take a mental note of the changes that are occurring around you. This is the beginning of the molting process. We can't react effectively if we fail to acknowledge the awareness we need to adapt.

Stillness

Just like in nature, animals initiating the molting process become still, literally ceasing to move about normally. We too, must allow the time for stillness and introspection. Being still allows for reflection on where we've been and where we have yet to go. More importantly, it gives us a head start on our mission to seize the next moment or venture with bravery.

Vulnerability

During the molting phase in nature, insects are totally vulnerable to predators due to the softness of their developing new outer shell. This mimics the vulnerability we all must sometimes face when we're developing and preparing ourselves for new phases. We may even find ourselves open to the opinions and feedback of others. However, what we stand to gain is far greater than any form of criticism. After all, no one can fully understand the potential that lies in your molting process.

Allow Room for Growth

When the molting process is complete, insects still must continue to expand their new covering, so it is big enough to create space for continued growth. As we develop new mental shells and approaches to our changing world, we too must continue to expand our perspective *and scope. Doing so allows for sustained agility and adaptability as we leverage new viewpoints and opportunities.*

Molting takes hard work, sometimes occurring over the span of a few hours to even days. We all undergo some form of it at various points in our personal and professional lives. The beauty lies in the ability for us to seize and capitalize on the awareness molting brings. As you continue adopting new ways of functioning in our ever-evolving world, acknowledge the changes and embrace the molt.

Do You Fight It or Do You Embrace the Molt?

Think about a time when you were going through the very uncomfortable *molting process,* trying to hold onto the old but knowing it was time to move onto the new.

Maybe you were leaving an old job, relationship, house, or situation that was no longer serving your highest good.

Jack Welch once said, **"Change before you have to."**

The older I get, the more I see that if we don't proactively change when it's time to, the Universe will often force us into it.

Two decades ago, I knew in my heart, mind, and soul that it was time to leave the legal field, but it had been my identity for 17 years and my survival, so I didn't take action.

Serendipitously, I was called into a meeting by the HR Department and told, "The department you work in is being restructured and your job no longer exists." It was actually code for: "You make too much money. You're fired!"

The point is, the change was long overdue. I needed to leave but was afraid to leave the safety and security of my job, so the Universe helped me out by getting me fired.

We all have this *Superpower to Molt*, but we can't hold onto the old and embrace the new; we have to choose one.

Letting Go Is Letting In

List three times in your life that you voluntarily or involuntarily Molted:

1. _____

2. _____

3. _____

These aren't the only times you will molt. There will always be more because of the endless and infinite Life/Death/Life cycle.

In her book, *Women Who Run with the Wolves,* author Clarissa Pinkola Estes, Ph.D., says:

> *The Life/Death/Life forces are part of our own nature, part of an inner authority that knows the steps, knows the dance of Life and Death. It is composed of the aspects of ourselves who know when something can, should, and must be born and what it must die. It is a deep teacher, if we can only learn its tempo.*

Life Is the Creating of Death

Lady Death surfaces whether we like it or not. We cannot run away from her forever; she will hunt us down.

As Dr. Estes points out, "This teacher comes whenever the soul calls – and thank goodness, for the ego is never fully ready."

The teacher may come in the form of getting fired from a job, a relationship ending unexpectedly, the death of someone, an illness, or a financial crisis.

When these events are happening, you can be sure the soul is calling for you to change.

How Do We Know When It's Time to Change?

When change is being thrust upon us.

Just like the lobster and the crayfish, it's not a one-and-done event.

You can make it a daily practice of looking at the Life/Death/Life nature over and over again by asking these questions that Dr. Estes lays out in her book:

- What must I give more death to today in order to generate more life?

- What do I know should die but am hesitant to allow to do so?

- What should die today?

- What should live?

- What life am I afraid to give birth to? If not now, when?

Meeting Billy Ray Cyrus helped me transition from my legal career to my writing career and being an entrepreneur. There was a huge death of my old identity and who I had been for 17 years, but eventually, new life emerged, as it always does.

There is true power and wisdom when you know the Life/Death/Life cycle and embrace it. Deep inside, we know when Lady Death is knocking at our door for something to change.

We must learn to trust it and know that when there is an ending, there will soon be another beginning.

Embrace Your Molt. It's your Superpower.

SUPERPOWER #4
THE POWER OF SIMMERING

Simmering is not the same as doing nothing. Simmering allows you to gather the strength you'll need to complete an activity. Every one of us has had the experience of becoming dramatically more productive after a period of simmering.

Everyone has a different simmering style... Whatever it is, give yourself permission to be "unproductive." We all need to simmer from time to time. It gives us strength to become boundlessly creative and wildly innovative.

– Chin-Ning Chu, *The Art of War for Women*

Angel Betty Rae, my 84-year-old bestselling author client, told me years ago that when you start "efforting," it's time to walk away from whatever you're doing and do something completely different. Her rule is "NO Efforting."

We've been trained to be productive and busy; however, overworking and overdoing can have negative consequences – like burnout.

When I left the legal field, it was hard for me to relax. It's like I had one speed, and that was high gear. It took about a year for me to ease into a lower gear and allow myself to relax and to just *be*.

Tama Kieves, a Harvard graduate and high-powered lawyer who left her thriving legal career to follow her dreams of writing and teaching, has a chapter in her book, *This Time I Dance*, called **"The Year of Sleeping Dangerously."** She describes that year like this:

> *After I walked out of my high-paced, breathless career, I functioned at what seemed to be two notches above the living dead line. I waited tables, bought groceries, and fed my cat. But I slept for what seemed to be an unnatural numbers of hours. My mind revved up like an eager sports car engine racing with the need to create a new and improved life. But I found my physical self dragging around the apartment in slow motion in my underwear in the middle of the day, then taking naps to recuperate. I felt like a beached whale hungering for the sea. I ate bagels and cream cheese and leftovers and lunchmeats instead. Guilt took finky little notes about my attraction to the refrigerator and shared them hourly…*

> [She wrote in her journal] *You did not leave a job to find a job, but to find yourself, the Queen you locked away, while you served lesser things and others' kings.*

> *I slept because I mourned the death or loss of an identity.*

Tama was taking a long and overdue *simmer* that her soul needed after the draining years of working extended hours to become a partner at a law firm.

She was in the season of "undoing" and it required every ounce of strength, vision, and persistence she had. The old way she had done things created a life she did NOT want. She had to *undo* an intact identity, which is a process that can take weeks, months, or in some cases (like hers), years.

I know I was restless after getting fired from the law firm. I had tons of time to myself but didn't know what to do with this unfamiliar free time. I, too, had lost my identity of being a paralegal and a corporate, 9-5 working woman.

This Down Time Can Feel Like Jell-O That Hasn't Quite Gelled. It Will Eventually, but We Are Impatient, and We Want It Now.

Sometimes we go through different versions of ourselves before hitting our authentic range. It's like going to a store and trying on a dozen different outfits to find that perfect one.

As Tama suggests, "It's just that we have to test our voices before we know the notes to sing."

It's a catch-22. To be ourselves we often are exiled by many people in our lives; yet if we comply with what others want, then we are exiled from ourselves.

So, we have a choice – be what others want and need us to be or choose ourselves.

Sometimes the Queen Chameleon has to step down from her throne and stop trying to fit in and please everyone.

It's draining not being yourself.

Giving yourself the gift of simmering will provide that self-connection you need to make superior choices in your life.

Think about the nine months of gestation required for a baby to develop in the mother's womb fully. We, too, need *Womb Time* to feed a precious new life. We need space to reclaim our strength and vision.

Do You Embrace Downtime or Do You Fight It in The Name of Being Productive and Busy?

We have two choices when we're in transition:

1. Giving yourself time to simmer; just *being* without taking action.

2. Trying to force something to happen.

In his book, *Power vs. Force,* Dr. David Hawkins says:

> Man thinks he lives by virtue of the forces he can control, but in fact, he's governed by power from unrevealed sources, power over which he has no control. Because power is effortless, it goes

unseen and unsuspected. Force is experienced through the sense; power can be recognized only through inner awareness.

My interpretation of that statement is that our power can only be found through inner awareness. David Hawkins goes on to say:

Facts are accumulated by effort, but truth reveals itself effortlessly.

I guess Angel Betty Rae was right – No efforting!

How Does One Stop Efforting and Allow More Time for Simmering?

The answer is: Presence.

In Zen, they call this *Satori,* which means a moment of *presence* – a brief stepping out of the voice in your head.

Eckhart Tolle, in his book, *A New Earth*, says:

The thinking mind cannot understand Presence and so will often misinterpret it… In the stillness of presence, you can sense the formless essence in yourself…

Meditation is a Tool That Helped Me Find Presence and The Inner Connection I Needed to Create A New Life.

I had a tremendous amount of anxiety after leaving the legal field because I felt guilty for not being at work and having all this free time. My mind was going a mile a minute, and one day, I ended up in the emergency room, believing I had a heart attack.

After all the heart tests came back negative, and they determined I had high amounts of stress causing anxiety, I was referred to a psychiatrist.

The doctor told me the only option I had was medication. I informed him, "I don't take pills," and inquired about what else I could do. His reply was, "Suffer."

I'm glad I didn't take him at his word. Luckily, I went to the bookstore and found a book on meditation that completely changed my life.

I Chose Meditation Over Medication

My anxiety slowly dissipated, and it hasn't been an issue since incorporating daily meditation into my life over 20 years ago.

Michael Singer, the author of *The Untethered Soul*, says this about our minds:

> *Your inner growth is completely dependent upon the realization that the only way to find peace and contentment is to stop thinking about yourself. You're ready to grow when you finally realize that the "I" who is always talking inside will never be content. It always has a problem with something. Honestly, when was the last time you really had nothing bothering you? Before you had your current problem, there was a different problem.*

The bottom line is you'll never be free of problems until you are free from the part within that has so many issues.

You have two distinct aspects of your inner being. The first is you, the awareness, the witness, the center of your willful intentions, and the other is that which you want. The problem is the part that you watch which never shuts up. If you could get rid of that part, even for a moment, the peace and serenity would be the nicest vacation you've ever had.

We all need a vacation from the constant chatter that goes on in our minds from the time we wake up until the time our eyes shut, and we go to sleep.

Michael calls this voice our inner roommate/inner troublemaker (IR/IT) and says we need to fire our IR/IT if we ever want to have peace, harmony, and quiet in our lives.

Meditation helped me quiet down my own IR/IT and connect with my deeper self.

Meditation is the return to the root of your being and the simple awareness of being aware.

We free ourselves by finding ourselves, and the way to find ourselves is to *simmer*. To just *be*. To be with the stillness and the inner self that doesn't have a problem with anything and knows that **all "problems" are agents for growth.**

When the bodyguard told us to leave the hotel and threatened to call security, I withdrew to the elevator and simmered for a bit. As I simmered, the thought popped into my head to pick up the house phone on the nearby table and call the number on the sign in front of me.

That's what not *efforting* and *simmering* does – it gives us the exact answer and action we need to take.

Allow yourself as much time as you need to *simmer*.

Once you simmer, you'll know exactly what you need to do in your life to get what you want.

This leads us to the next chapter, the Lost Art of Wanting…

SUPERPOWER #5
THE LOST ART OF WANTING

I bet if I asked you what you ***don't want*** in your life, you could give me a pretty big list of things:

- I don't want my boring job
- I don't want to clean up after everyone all the time
- I don't want to argue with my partner anymore
- I don't want to get up at 6 a.m. and commute to work every day
- I don't want to deal with this problem client
- … and the list goes on and on.

Dr. Helene Brenner, in her book, *I Know I'm In There Somewhere*, says:

> *Don't-wants tend to be very loud. And they certainly are a form of WANTING. But by themselves, they rarely move you.*
>
> *That's because they only lead away from something, not toward something. No wonder don't-wants don't fill us up. Don't-wants are familiar, safe, and comfortable. You're already living with them. Wanting is more challenging. It takes you out of what you're familiar with into new territory.*

> *Many women believe it's bad or wrong or irresponsible or unspiritual to want.*

It's Time to Claim Your Wants

There is power in wanting because you set an intention to move towards something rather than away from something.

There are two kinds of wants – *possible* wants and *impossible* wants. Both serve their purpose.

It's essential to make a list of both types of wants because it's an exercise in listening to our inner self and validating her.

In my book, **<u>How to Find Your Passion: 23 Questions That an Change Your Entire Life</u>**, there is a powerful question:

If I Had $10 Million Dollars in the Bank, I Would…

That question forces you to think outside the box and really allow yourself to Dream Big. I'm going through my book right now as a daily practice and answering the questions; that specific question is challenging. It made me pause and think about what I would be doing differently in my life with $10 million dollars in the bank than what I'm doing now.

Money gives us more freedom and options, which is why this is such a great question. You may not have that freedom right now, but if you allow yourself to Dream Big, you may find repressed desires that you haven't thought about for years.

Make a List of 10 Wants Including Possible and Impossible Ones

Don't focus on "how" these things could happen – allow yourself to want without limitations or knowing how to get it.

We lose our **Superpower of Wanting** when we don't want to feel or acknowledge those wants and desires because we're afraid if we do, then we might be disappointed if we don't get them.

It's better to play it safe and *not* want things we're unsure we can get or that seem impossible.

After I left the legal field, working 40+ hours per week and making $50,000 a year, I bought a book by Barbara Stanny, *Secrets of Six-Figure Women*. Honestly, I never thought about making six figures before I read that book. I was stuck in survival mode, living paycheck-to-paycheck.

Barbara interviewed over 150 six-figure women and wrote about the common characteristics of these six figure earners. Reading that book inspired me and helped me believe in myself more. As I was reading it, I thought to myself, "If these women can do it, so can I." Within 18 months of reading that book, I was making six figures working 25 hours per week in an outside sales job.

I remember, writing daily affirmations for months after I read her book:

I Am Making Six Figures Doing What I Love.

I didn't focus on the *how*; I focused on the desire to make six figures instead and how that would change my life. I would never have imagined that I could make six figures working in outside sales – selling hot tubs – since I had zero sales experience.

We must focus on the *desire* more than the path to get there. That's where mystery, synchronicity, and faith come in. If you can believe it, you can achieve it.

When you write down a desire, if a negative feeling comes up like *this is impossible, it can never happen*; that feeling is hiding your fear of wanting for and believing in yourself.

Acknowledge the Fear and the Feeling, but Don't Feed it or Give it Power

We all fear change because our lizard brain wants to keep us living in the status quo; change is scary and dangerous. What if we become wealthy and the people in our lives don't love us anymore?

Our Inner Troublemaker wants to find problems with everything. Don't allow it to. Yes, when we change, people sometimes exit our lives.

Yet, when we believe in ourselves, we know we can handle anything that comes our way, including people leaving our lives for whatever reason.

My best friend from middle school and high school distanced herself from me after I started making money and becoming more successful. I think it was a painful reminder that she was still struggling financially, and nothing was changing in her own life. She complained about the same "money issues" for 35 years.

For years, we bonded over being broke and living paycheck-to-paycheck. As I started having more financial success, she slowly disappeared from my life.

That's okay. It was an adjustment, but I accepted it and I was able to handle it. Remember, in the Life/Death/Life cycle, when there is a death, new life always appears.

Now, I have a new best friend who is financially successful and always growing and evolving. He's an amazing person, and I probably wouldn't have him in my life if my other friendship had not been removed.

By Changing, You Will Inspire Others

Molting and changing is scary, but we can also be a role model and an inspiration to other people when we get to the other side.

Just like Barbara Stanny's personal story and the stories of those 150 women inspired me to believe in myself and become bigger than I was, so can your story.

From Your List of 10 Wants, Write a New Story Three Years From Now Living Your New Life

Without the carrot on the stick (our desires and wants), we would remain stagnant and not grow. To make six figures, I had to grow on many different levels.

Allow yourself to want, to write your new story, and then allow the universe to guide you on the path to making all of your dreams come true.

Here's an Innercize from Dr. Brenner's book called *The Ten Degree Change*:

> *Take an area of your life where getting what you want seems "impossible." Now brainstorm ways that you can get a little of what you want. Just ten degrees, or even one degree, of it. If you're in a house with a fifties-style kitchen that you can't stand and can't afford to remodel, go to a store and pick out the tile that you'll one day retile it with, buy one tile, and put it next to the wall. Any little thing you can do to move toward the direction of your want and feel good. Repeat this Innercize often.*

A while back, I wanted new carpeting for my family room because the carpet that came with the house was stained and worn out. I went to the carpet store and picked out a beautiful new carpet with a high price tag. I got a sample and put it on the fireplace mantel so I could look at it every day and imagine the new carpeting in my family room.

About a year went by when a friend told me about a carpet warehouse that had wholesale prices. I took a trip out there and found the exact carpet I wanted for less than half of the carpet store's price. I bought it and was so happy to have this beautiful new carpet in my family room.

Look at your list of wants above, and next to each one, write down your ten-degree action you can take now.

Don't wait until you can have the whole thing. Set your intention and take small actions towards your desires, which leads us to our next chapter and next Superpower, *Dream Big, Start Small…*

SUPERPOWER #6
DREAM BIG, START SMALL

I am all for dreaming big. However, when we allow ourselves to dream big, our brains want to know the exact steps to get there. Once we go into *analysis mode* and try to figure it ALL out, we become overwhelmed, eventually causing enough stress and anxiety to convince ourselves to stop going after that big dream.

In this chapter, we will identify one BIG dream for you and discuss some small steps you can take to move toward that big dream.

Years ago, I attended a health fair and met an interesting lady that did readings. At the time, I didn't even know what a *reading* was, but she told me I could ask her anything and she would give me the answer.

I asked her, "Why do I always pick the wrong men?"

Her reply was, "You have a neon sign on your crotch that says CLOSED FOR BUSINESS with a very small opening for men to get in, like a tiny window. And the only thing that can fit through that tiny window are snakes, worms, little insects...things you really don't want."

Then, she stood next to me and said, "I want you to look around the room at the men here. Do you see that man, he's a possibility, and that one over there, he's a possibility, and that one over there, he's a possibility. Notice I didn't say probability; I said possibility. You have to open your eyes and look at all the possibilities."

At that point in my life, I just avoided men. I would not even look in their direction and focused on other areas in my life instead. But eventually, one of those snakes would get my attention and wiggle their way into my tiny window, causing a great deal of harm and destruction.

Avoidance can work for a while, but it's not a long-term strategy.

What If We Don't Know What Our Dream Is Or We Have So Many It's Overwhelming?

Rachel Hollis, in her book *Girl, Stop Apologizing*, says the following about dreams:

> *Choose one dream and go all in. This one is aimed at all my dreamers who are like, I want to author a book, but I'm also a singer-songwriter and I'm thinking about getting my real estate license and I also want to work with homeless animals and start a charity to bring endangered species into senior citizens' homes to comfort the aged.*
>
> *No.*

> *First, even if your list isn't quite so elaborate, even if all the things on it support one another, even then, it's not going to be effective. If it were effective, it would have worked already.*
>
> *Second, that list isn't one filled with dreams. That is a list filled with some cool ideas. You need to understand the difference.*
>
> *When I say dream, I mean something you greatly desire. I mean that you're fantasizing about something and imagining what it would be like regularly. I mean that when you think about it your heart beats fast and your palms get sweaty...*
>
> *Back to the dream versus great idea thing. When people list nineteen things they're dreaming of, my response is always the same: Which one makes you most excited? If you could choose only one of them to work on for the next decade, which would it be? If only one of them could be successful, which one would you choose?*

It's time to learn how to separate cool ideas from having a single, focused dream.

Ideas are a dime a dozen. It's fun to have a lot of cool ideas; however, this can be disguised as having "dreams" since the options and possibilities are limitless. This way, if chasing the dream becomes hard and challenging (like when the obstacles show up), then we can quit and say we really didn't want it. Besides, we have so many other *cool ideas*.

Are you starting to see the difference?

It's very similar to the *Lost Art of Wanting*. It's easy to make a list of what we don't want. It's safer, but it rarely moves us forward because there is no intention or specificity about what we do want.

Thinking back on my desire to be an attorney when I was 17 years old, that was my dream. But there were many obstacles and I gave up on that dream and chose Plan B instead, which was becoming a paralegal.

If we have no Plan B, then chances are greater that we will actually realize our *Plan A* dream once we identify it.

The night I pursued Billy Ray Cyrus, I had no Plan B; I was going to do whatever it took to meet him even if I ended up in jail. I know it sounds a little crazy, but to achieve great things, you need a bit of crazy.

I recommend the book *Can't Hurt Me* by David Goggins. He shares on his website what he has achieved, and a lot of people call him crazy:

> *David Goggins is a retired Navy SEAL and is the only member of the U.S. Armed Forces to complete SEAL training (including two Hell Weeks), the U.S. Army Ranger School (where he graduated as an Enlisted Honor Man) and Air Force Tactical Air Controller training.*

An accomplished endurance athlete, Goggins has completed over 60 ultra-marathons, triathlons, and ultra-triathlons, setting new course records and regularly placing in the top five. He once held the Guinness World Record for pull-ups completing 4,030 in 17 hours, and he's a sought after public speaker.

Goggins says, "The pain that you are willing to endure is measured by how bad you want it."

Having a Plan B is Dangerous – It Gives You an Out

If you want to take control of the island, you have to burn the boats. Although that is a war analogy, it works when you are going after your dreams; don't give yourself an out.

As women, we love having a buffet of choices; we don't want to be limited to only one option. But here's the thing, when you chase two rabbits, you get none.

When we are chasing too many things and are not focused, our energy becomes scattered.

In his book *Essentialism: The Disciplined Pursuit of Less*, author Greg McKeown, says when we have too many choices, we suffer from decision fatigue. He says we can learn to make one-time decisions that will make a thousand future decisions, so we don't exhaust ourselves asking the same question again and again.

He includes the following great drawing in his book that conveys this message beautifully:

How effective can we be when our energy is scattered as in the illustration on the left? When we make a choice to focus on one dream, then we can focus all of our attention and energy on that *one thing*.

If you don't prioritize your life, someone else will, and that someone else might be your family, boss, partner, or society.

We have so many choices now in our lives compared to generations before us, and we have become overwhelmed in our ability to manage them. Many of us suffer from decision fatigue, which means the more choices we are forced to make, the more the quality of our decisions deteriorates.

You might be wondering, "Can we have it all?"

My answer is, "Maybe, but not all at once."

I think it's good to explore and evaluate what you want, but eventually, you have to choose one thing to focus on.

Greg McKeown's process is:

1. Explore and Evaluate
2. Eliminate
3. Execute

McKeown says, "Everything changes when we permit ourselves to be more selective in what we choose to do. At once, we hold the key to unlock the next level of achievement in our lives."

It may seem like we are giving up on our list of "cool ideas" or "dreams", but we're not. Instead, we're choosing to focus on one at a time for maximum leverage and efficiency.

Everything Matters Equally is a Lie

Gary Keller, author of *The One Thing*, says:

> *Equality is a lie.*
>
> *Understanding this is the basis of all great decisions.*
>
> *When everything feels urgent and important, everything seem equal. We stay active and busy, but this doesn't actually move us any closer to success. Activity is often unrelated to productivity, and busyness rarely takes care of business.*

Keller recommends using a *Success List* instead of a *To-Do* List. "To-Do Lists tend to be long; Success Lists are short. One pulls you in all directions; the other aims you in a specific direction."

Here are the steps to creating your own Success List:

- **Go small**. Don't focus on being busy; focus on being productive. Allow what matters most to drive your day.

- **Go extreme**. Once you've figured out what actually matters, keep asking what matters most until there is only one thing left. That core activity goes at the top of your success list.

- **Say no**. Whether you say "later" or "never," the point is to say "not now" to anything else you could do until your most important work is done.

- Don't get trapped in the "check off" game. If we believe things don't matter equally, we must act accordingly.

Gary also suggests this very powerful focusing question:

"What's the ONE thing I can do such that by doing it, everything else will be easier or unnecessary?"

Pretty amazing question, right?

Let's do an exercise and choose ONE Dream to focus on.

To do that, I want you to write about the *future you* ten years from now.

Here are some questions to answer when writing about your future self:

- Where does she live?
- What is her presence like?
- What does she do with her time?
- What does her day look like?
- Who is she surrounded by?
- Where does she live?
- What time does she get up?
- What time does she go to bed?
- What does her home look like?
- What does she eat?
- How does she make a living?
- Does she travel?
- What are her hobbies?
- What are her spiritual practices?
- How does she give back?
- What kind of clothes does she wear?
- How does she rest?
- How does she approach life?
- What message does she have for the younger you now?

Your *future self* can give you hints about what you need to focus on now and what your dream is. She's not just an "older in age" version of you; she is a wiser guide who can mentor you now.

Once you finish the "Future Self" exercise, I want you to write down whatever "dreams" came to you. List up to ten.

1. _____
2. _____
3. _____
4. _____
5. _____
6. _____
7. _____
8. _____
9. _____
10. _____

What is the one goal or thing you can do that will get you closer to the future version of yourself the fastest?

Write down the specific goal and describe how you will measure your progress.

Pick one goal to focus on, not ten. Then, write down small steps you can take now.

How I am Able to Write a Book a Month

When I decided I wanted to earn six figures in passive income from my writing, I committed to write one book per month for a year. To achieve that goal, I had to eliminate a lot from my life – from social activities to other goals and dreams. I had to give a good portion of my energy and time to this dream, and I'm happy to tell you, it has paid off enormously. It hasn't always been easy, and there have been many obstacles (like my 30-year-old daughter and 2-year-old granddaughter moving in with me temporarily for one year during the lock-down), but I didn't let anything stop me.

Burn the Boats, and Burn Your Plan B

Remember the *Power of Simmering* we talked about earlier. Once you choose a dream or goal to focus on, give yourself some time to simmer on it and make sure you are aligned with it; that it really connects with your heart, mind, and soul. If not, choose a different goal.

I know so many people who say they want to write books; most of them never do because it's hard work. Read Steven Pressfield's book, *The War of Art*, where he talks about the *Resistance* showing up to stop you from writing, and you'll understand what I mean.

The resistance is real, but when we have a *future self* we want to live in to, things become clearer about the steps we can take now.

The Difference Between Men and Women

Last year, a high-powered tax attorney booked a strategy session with me inquiring about my Bestselling Author program. We got to chatting about the differences between coaching men and women, and she said something like this:

> *The way I see it, if I tell a man to go out and make a million dollars in six months, he'll come back to me having achieved the goal and then some. He probably screwed up a hundred times, tried numerous things to make it happen, and didn't know what the heck he was doing.*
>
> *When I give women the same instructions, they often come back to me not hitting the goal (maybe they make $10) and giving me a litany of reasons why they didn't hit the goal – well, I had to get this certification, and I had to take this course, and I had to read these books, and I needed a new website, and I had to get a logo, and I needed the blessing of so and so….yada yada yada.*
>
> *The bottom line is this…men I have to rein in and women I have to push off the ledge.*

She reminded me of something that happened when I was first starting in the online space, going from being a 9-5 employee to an entrepreneur. I spent an excessive amount of time (one year) getting my first website built. I was indecisive about colors, logos, themes, wording, etc. A year later, I still had no website.

Around that time, I attended a workshop and asked the workshop leader what she thought my website's colors and theme should be.

Her reply was, "Michelle, it's not about the colors, the theme, the design, or any of that. You're afraid to be found."

Wow! She was absolutely right. Deep inside, I had a lot of fears about being in the public eye where I would be vulnerable to judgment, criticism, and unreasonable expectations from others. I was terrified, so I used the distraction of the "website" to prevent me from moving forward and achieving my goal and dream – making a living with my online business.

I've had many teachers along the way who have steered me in the right direction and helped me uncover my hidden fears as well as my secret desires.

If you're busy all the time, and haven't achieved your dreams or goals, you are probably *majoring in minor activities*. It seems like you're busy, but you're concentrating on the wrong activities.

Or you're trying to have it all and are pursuing the goal of more, more, more.

In the book, *Essentialism*, that I mentioned earlier, Greg explains why having our Top 10 Priorities list doesn't work:

> *The word priority came into the English language in the 1400's. It was singular. It meant the very first or prior thing. It stayed singular for the next five hundred years.*

> *Only in the 1900's did we pluralize the term and start talking about priorities. Illogically, we reasoned that by changing the word we could bend reality. Somehow, we would now be able to have multiple "first" things. People and companies routinely try to do just that. One leader told me of his experience in a company that talked of "Pri-1, Pri-2, Pri-3, Pri-4 and Pri-5." This gave the impression of many things being the priority but actually meant nothing was.*

I found this story fascinating and meaningful. If we have our top 10 priorities, and we are trying to have it all at once, then we will find ourselves making trade-offs at the margins, which we probably would not have taken on as a deliberate strategy.

This is why we must select one priority at a time. Once we have identified that priority, we will place all of our attention, energy and focus on making it happen.

We'll be operating from the illustration on the right from Greg's book, *Essentialism*, instead of the one on the left.

Your Superpower is *Dreaming Big*, just like when you were a little girl. You dreamed about flying over the trees in your neighborhood, about having exotic tea parties with fairies and being the queen of your castle. All BIG Dreams are made of small steps that will get us there at the perfect time. Whatever your dream is, you can begin today with one small step.

My dream was to meet Billy Ray Cyrus, and achieving that dream connected me to my bigger dream of becoming a writer. Without meeting Billy Ray, I might not have found that buried dream. I took action on my goal, and that made all the difference.

The next Superpower is taking Double Jumps towards your dreams.

SUPERPOWER #7
DOUBLE JUMPING

We can have the biggest dream in the world, but without action, it will remain an unrealized dream. Inspired action is the goal.

Taking small steps is great because it is progress, but there are also ways to fast-track your goals and dreams.

Think About the Game of Checkers...

The goal is to move your pieces across the checkerboard while jumping over your opponent's pieces so you can remove them all from the board and win.

When you are playing checkers, you are sometimes given the opportunity to double jump your opponent's checkers. According to the blog, *Checkers Lounge*, a double jump is this:

A checkers double jump is simply defined as being a move where two jumps are made one after the other within a single turn. The end result of this single move is that a player can capture two of the opponent's checkers pieces at once. A checkers double jump is possible if, after making a single jump that results in a capture, the very same checkers piece is in a position to make yet another capture. This subsequent move can either be along the same diagonal direction or it may move off into another direction.

You can win the game a lot faster if you get the chance to do some double jumping.

We Need Double Jumps to Achieve Our Dreams

Let me give you an example. Earlier, I mentioned the book *Can't Hurt Me* by David Goggins, a self-published book by an unknown author that hit the New York Times bestsellers list and has gone on to sell millions of copies.

How did this happen?

Joe Rogan, standup comedian, and host of one of the top-rated podcasts, *The Joe Rogan Experience*, interviewed Goggins. Rogan has millions of followers, and Goggins' book took off after the interview. That interview has almost 7,000,000 views as of the date of this writing.

Goggins did a "quadruple jump" to achieve book sales and reach millions of people with his incredible story.

When you fully commit to your #1 goal and singular priority, think about how to include double jumps, triple jumps, and quadruple jumps to achieve your goals. Some of these jumps will happen mysteriously and organically; however, you can also intentionally cause them to happen.

Goggins fast-tracked his goals by being interviewed on a podcast with millions of viewers and subscribers.

If we stay on the slow path too long, it may be because we are unknowingly delaying and hiding, like I was when I wasted a year attempting to have a website created. The thing you DON'T want to do is often the thing you need to do.

Some of the actions we need to take are inherently slow and require diligence, discipline, and patience. Other actions are delays, fears, and distractions in disguise.

Are You Really Giving It Your All?

Goggins says we often think we're operating at 100% and giving it our all, but most people are really only giving about 40%. We naturally stop doing things when we experience pain, suffering, and discomfort. But if you want to change your life in a big way, you have to get past that 40% mark.

My first book, *Quit Your Job and Follow Your Dreams,* took me almost two years to write. I didn't have deadlines or a plan of action; it was just an idea to write a book and get it published. It was a slow and painful process.

After stretching it out and causing myself a lot of undue suffering, I finally published that book. I don't wish on anyone. When clients hire me for my done-for-you bestselling author program, they often tell me they've spent one, two, five, or sometimes ten years working on their book.

Deciding in January 2020 to write a book a month was one of the best things I've ever done. It started when I read an article by

Written Word Media[1] that said the average author earning $100k per year has 28 books in their catalog. I immediately decided I was going to write a book a month and test this theory.

Before writing a book a month, I thought I was operating at 100% because I was publishing approximately 50 books per year for clients. I didn't see how I could find the time to write, publish, and launch my own books. I was wrong, though. The time I needed to write a book a month was buried in my excuses and lack of focus. To achieve this goal, I had to make writing a book a month my #1 and only priority for the next year.

Now I'm skeptical when people say a good book takes time and then spend years writing while I know that they're lying to themselves. I say a "good enough" book takes 30 days.

In my book a month schedule that I set for myself, I don't have time to waste time. I can't lie to myself and say the book isn't perfect yet because I know it never will be perfect. It just has to be *good enough*.

Seth Godin, a prolific author of many books on sales and marketing says, *"It doesn't ship because it's ready. It ships because it's due."*

When you have all the time in the world to do something, you often don't get it done.

---

[1] https://www.writtenwordmedia.com/author-income-how-to-make-a-living-from-your-writing/

Parkinson's Law Is 100% Correct

Parkinson's law states, "Work expands to fill the time available for its completion."

I heard about this law before, but now I believe it at the core of my being since I began writing a book a month. This book you are reading is my tenth book this year (2020). This book would never have been written if I didn't have the "book a month" deadline, schedule, and system driving me every month.

Did you ever notice that when you're about to go on vacation and you have to finish up all the loose ends at work, all of a sudden, you're like Super Woman and you get a week's worth of work done in a few hours? Amazing, right?

That's Parkinson's law at work.

So now that you have your #1 Goal/Dream that you are going to focus on, what are some ways you can take a double jump?

Tara Mohr, in her book, *Playing Big*, says this about leaping:

> *Writing a list of one's passion is not a leap! In fact, it's designing at the whiteboard, assuming you have to make the perfect choice (or that you can make the perfect choice) of what direction to pursue while sitting in isolation at your desk and thinking hard about it. Classic hiding strategy!* **Leaping is about learning via doing—not trying to figure it out.**

Our minds will come up with infinite ways to distract, delay, and avoid reaching our dreams because its goal is to keep us safe and avoid pushing the status quo. Our Inner Troublemaker will tell us that it's a dangerous world when you take action and try to change your life. Just remember, it's also dangerous to remain stagnant.

We're born to evolve and grow and not to remain stagnant. Just like the blue crawfish who was molting away from the shell that had become too small to house her, you can't stay in the same shell forever.

When the soul is ready to change, you'll know. You can listen and make changes or you'll be forced to make changes.

I see so many authors deluding themselves as they waste months and years planning out their book and see that as *action*. Yes, a book does take time to plan out (and it used to take me months). Now, it takes me three days because I have a deadline, a system, and a very specific goal – write a book a month.

When I hit roadblocks and obstacles trying to meet Billy Ray, I used the power of simmering to see what my next course of action would be. I didn't simmer too long though because I would have lost momentum and possibly courage. The key is I took inspired action; I didn't just think about what to do – I did it.

Some dreams and goals inherently seem impossible. If that's the case, break it down into manageable steps. Usually, when you take a step in the right direction, another door will mysteriously open up.

The Magic of 51

I don't remember where I heard this because it was so long ago, but it makes sense. Consider the amount of energy and action it takes to complete a goal is 100%.

Here's how it works:

- You move 10% towards your goal, and the universe moves 10%

- You move 20% towards your goal, and the universe moves 20%

- You move 30% towards your goal, and the universe moves 30%

- You move 40% towards your goal, and the universe moves 40%

Here's where the *magic* kicks in…

When you move 51% towards your goal, the universe moves the other 49%, and your goal is complete.

Until you have moved 51%, you are just "involved" in your goal and not fully committed. The threshold for commitment is 51%, and that is the point that the universe knows you are serious and moves in to help you realize your goal.

When I see others fail to achieve a goal, it's usually because they quit at the 10%, 20%, 30% or 40% involvement stage. I think it's interesting that Goggins says people are only operating at 40% capacity but believe they are operating at 100%.

Magic happens when you move 51% towards your goal.

I'll end this chapter with one of my favorite quotes:

> *"When you're on a journey to fulfill your personal legend, the whole universe conspires to help you achieve it."*
>
> **~Paulo Coehlo,** *The Alchemist*

Use your Double Jumping Superpower and don't apologize for it. Remember, you're fulfilling your personal legend.

CLOSING THOUGHTS

You have a lot more than Seven Superpowers, and this book was written to remind you of some of them.

I was listening to an interview with former Secret Service Agent Evy Poumpouras, author of *Becoming Bulletproof,* and at the end of the interview,[2] the host asked her, "What's your Superpower?"

She replied, "I fail a lot. Failure is my Superpower. The more I fail, the more resilient I become, and the less afraid I am of it."

Wow! That blew me away because we're so conditioned to being afraid to fail that we shrink and give up before we even have a chance to succeed.

Failure is one of our Superpowers, and I will remind myself of that every day.

Let me ask you a question.

I published ten books so far this year, and three of them are generating 80% of my income from book royalties, which currently is around $2,300 per month.

---

[2] https://www.youtube.com/watch?v=loG9ujz0N4M&feature=youtu.be

Does that mean the other seven books are failures because they are not selling as many?

In my opinion, they are not failures. When you create content for public consumption, you do not know what the market wants. Heck, they don't even know what they want until they see it. The world is rapidly changing, so something that might not have been popular yesterday, may be popular today.

I always tell my clients that the market decides what it likes and remind them that the market is fickle and always changing. All I can do is write quality, authentic books, put out the best product I can, stay true to myself and see what happens.

My other books that make up 20% of my income is actually bringing in over $500 per month. The primary goal for my books is to change lives; it's not all about the money.

I don't have a crystal ball to predict which books will sell, but success to me is not just the number of sales but transforming lives. I'm writing books because writing and teaching are my passion, and I feel that's what I was born to do.

Life Is Not Predictable

If you want answers before you begin on the journey to achieve your dreams, or you want a guarantee, then you're going to be disappointed. There are no guarantees.

When I got fired from my job at the law firm, my first goal was to pay my bills without a job. My next goal was to make six figures working half the hours. The goal after that was to get writing experience. Then my goal was to start an online business. After that, the goal was to make six figures from my online business. My newest goal is to write a book a month and make six figures from my royalties.

Having a goal is not a one-and-done event. It's like an onion; we are unpeeling layers that will take us to our next goal and the next season in our lives.

Each dream you have is just a beginning to the next step in your journey… and the steps are infinite.

I want to wish you well on your journey to becoming 100% authentic, embracing your **Red Dress Energy,** which you were born with, and letting the world see the real YOU!

Much love and success,

Michelle Kulp

Xxxxxooooo

Can You Do Me A Favor?

If you enjoyed this book or found it useful, I'd be very grateful if you'd post a short review on Amazon. Your support really does make a difference, and I read all the reviews personally to get your feedback and make this book even better.

Thanks again for your support!

www.ingramcontent.com/pod-product-compliance
Lightning Source LLC
LaVergne TN
LVHW051848080426
835512LV00018B/3131